THIS BOOK BELONGS TO :

....

....

Title : ....

Author : ....

Genre : ....

Start date : ....

End date : ....

Number of pages : ....

#1

BOOK FORMAT

◯ Physical book

◯ E-book

◯ Audio-book

MY REVIEW

....

....

....

....

....

....

....

....

....

....

....

....

....

....

TYPE OF BOOK

◯ fiction

◯ Non-fiction

WHY I READ IT

....

....

WHO WILL I RECOMMEND IT TO

....

....

RATING

☆ ☆ ☆ ☆ ☆

FAVORITE QUOTES   PAGE :

....

....

....

....

Title : ....

Author : ....

Genre : ....

Start date : ....

End date : ....

Number of pages : ....

#2

BOOK FORMAT

◯ Physical book

◯ E-book

◯ Audio-book

MY REVIEW

....

....

....

....

....

....

....

....

....

....

....

....

....

TYPE OF BOOK

◯ fiction

◯ Non-fiction

WHY I READ IT

....

....

WHO WILL I RECOMMEND IT TO

....

....

RATING

☆ ☆ ☆ ☆ ☆

FAVORITE QUOTES   PAGE

....

....

....

....

Title : ....

Author : ....

Genre : ....

Start date : ....

End date : ....

Number of pages : ....

#3

BOOK FORMAT

◯ Physical book

◯ E-book

◯ Audio-book

MY REVIEW

....
....
....
....
....
....
....
....
....
....
....
....
....
....
....

TYPE OF BOOK

◯ fiction

◯ Non-fiction

WHY I READ IT

....
....

WHO WILL I RECOMMEND IT TO

....
....

RATING

☆ ☆ ☆ ☆ ☆

FAVORITE QUOTES

PAGE :

....
....
....
....

Title : ....

Author : ....

Genre : ....

Start date : ....

End date : ....

Number of pages : ....

#4

BOOK FORMAT

◯ Physical book

◯ E-book

◯ Audio-book

MY REVIEW

....

....

....

....

....

....

....

....

....

....

....

....

....

TYPE OF BOOK

◯ fiction

◯ Non-fiction

WHY I READ IT

....

....

WHO WILL I RECOMMEND IT TO

....

....

RATING

☆ ☆ ☆ ☆ ☆

FAVORITE QUOTES   PAGE

....

....

....

....

Title : ....

Author : ....

Genre : ....

Start date : ....

End date : ....

Number of pages : ....

#5

BOOK FORMAT

◯ Physical book

◯ E-book

◯ Audio-book

MY REVIEW

....

....

....

....

....

....

....

....

....

....

....

....

....

TYPE OF BOOK

◯ fiction

◯ Non-fiction

WHY I READ IT

....

....

WHO WILL I RECOMMEND IT TO

....

....

RATING

☆ ☆ ☆ ☆ ☆

FAVORITE QUOTES   PAGE

....

....

....

....

Title : ....

Author : ....

Genre : ....

Start date : ....

End date : ....

Number of pages : ....

#6

BOOK FORMAT

◯ Physical book

◯ E-book

◯ Audio-book

MY REVIEW

....

....

....

....

....

....

....

....

....

....

....

....

....

....

TYPE OF BOOK

◯ fiction

◯ Non-fiction

WHY I READ IT

....

....

WHO WILL I RECOMMEND IT TO

....

....

RATING

☆ ☆ ☆ ☆ ☆

FAVORITE QUOTES   PAGE

....

....

....

....

Title : ....

Author : ....

Genre : ....

Start date : ....

End date : ....

Number of pages : ....

#7

BOOK FORMAT

◯ Physical book

◯ E-book

◯ Audio-book

MY REVIEW

....

....

....

....

....

....

....

....

....

....

....

....

....

....

....

TYPE OF BOOK

◯ fiction

◯ Non-fiction

WHY I READ IT

....

....

WHO WILL I RECOMMEND IT TO

....

....

RATING

☆☆☆☆☆

FAVORITE QUOTES   PAGE

....

....

....

....

Title : ....

Author : ....

Genre : ....

Start date : ....

End date : ....

Number of pages : ....

#8

BOOK FORMAT

◯ Physical book

◯ E-book

◯ Audio-book

MY REVIEW

....

....

....

....

....

....

....

....

....

....

....

....

....

....

....

....

TYPE OF BOOK

◯ fiction

◯ Non-fiction

WHY I READ IT

....

....

WHO WILL I RECOMMEND IT TO

....

....

RATING

☆ ☆ ☆ ☆ ☆

FAVORITE QUOTES   PAGE

....

....

....

....

Title : ....

Author : ....

Genre : ....

Start date : ....

End date : ....

Number of pages : ....

MY REVIEW

....

....

....

....

....

....

....

....

....

....

....

....

....

....

FAVORITE QUOTES

....

....

....

....

#9

BOOK FORMAT

◯ Physical book

◯ E-book

◯ Audio-book

TYPE OF BOOK

◯ fiction

◯ Non-fiction

WHY I READ IT

....

....

WHO WILL I RECOMMEND IT TO

....

....

RATING

☆ ☆ ☆ ☆ ☆

PAGE :

Title : ....

Author : ....

Genre : ....

Start date : ....

End date : ....

Number of pages : ....

BOOK FORMAT

◯ Physical book

◯ E-book

◯ Audio-book

MY REVIEW

....

....

....

....

....

....

....

....

....

....

....

....

....

TYPE OF BOOK

◯ fiction

◯ Non-fiction

WHY I READ IT

....

....

WHO WILL I RECOMMEND IT TO

....

....

RATING

☆ ☆ ☆ ☆ ☆

FAVORITE QUOTES   PAGE

....

....

....

....

Title : ....

Author : ....

Genre : ....

Start date : ....

End date : ....

Number of pages : ....

#11

BOOK FORMAT

◯ Physical book

◯ E-book

◯ Audio-book

MY REVIEW

....

....

....

....

....

....

....

....

....

....

....

....

....

....

TYPE OF BOOK

◯ fiction

◯ Non-fiction

WHY I READ IT

....

....

WHO WILL I RECOMMEND IT TO

....

....

RATING

☆ ☆ ☆ ☆ ☆

FAVORITE QUOTES   PAGE :

....

....

....

....

Title : ....

Author : ....

Genre : ....

Start date : ....

End date : ....

Number of pages : ....

#12

BOOK FORMAT

◯ Physical book

◯ E-book

◯ Audio-book

MY REVIEW

....

....

....

....

....

....

....

....

....

....

....

....

....

TYPE OF BOOK

◯ fiction

◯ Non-fiction

WHY I READ IT

....

....

WHO WILL I RECOMMEND IT TO

....

....

RATING

☆ ☆ ☆ ☆ ☆

FAVORITE QUOTES   PAGE

....

....

....

....

Title : ....

Author : ....

Genre : ....

Start date : ....

End date : ....

Number of pages : ....

#13

BOOK FORMAT

◯ Physical book

◯ E-book

◯ Audio-book

MY REVIEW

....

....

....

....

....

....

....

....

....

....

....

....

....

TYPE OF BOOK

◯ fiction

◯ Non-fiction

WHY I READ IT

....

....

WHO WILL I RECOMMEND IT TO

....

....

RATING

☆ ☆ ☆ ☆ ☆

FAVORITE QUOTES   PAGE :

....

....

....

....

Title : ....

Author : ....

Genre : ....

Start date : ....

End date : ....

Number of pages : ....

#14

BOOK FORMAT

◯ Physical book

◯ E-book

◯ Audio-book

MY REVIEW

....

....

....

....

....

....

....

....

....

....

....

....

....

....

TYPE OF BOOK

◯ fiction

◯ Non-fiction

WHY I READ IT

....

....

WHO WILL I RECOMMEND IT TO

....

....

RATING

☆ ☆ ☆ ☆ ☆

FAVORITE QUOTES   PAGE

....

....

....

....

Title : ....

Author : ....

Genre : ....

Start date : ....

End date : ....

Number of pages : ....

#15

BOOK FORMAT

◯ Physical book

◯ E-book

◯ Audio-book

TYPE OF BOOK

◯ fiction

◯ Non-fiction

MY REVIEW

....

....

....

....

....

....

....

....

....

....

....

....

....

....

WHY I READ IT

....

....

WHO WILL I RECOMMEND IT TO

....

....

RATING

☆ ☆ ☆ ☆ ☆

FAVORITE QUOTES   PAGE :

....

....

....

....

Title : ....

Author : ....

Genre : ....

Start date : ....

End date : ....

Number of pages : ....

#16

BOOK FORMAT

◯ Physical book

◯ E-book

◯ Audio-book

MY REVIEW

....
....
....
....
....
....
....
....
....
....
....
....
....
....

TYPE OF BOOK

◯ fiction

◯ Non-fiction

WHY I READ IT

....
....

WHO WILL I RECOMMEND IT TO

....
....

RATING

☆☆☆☆☆

FAVORITE QUOTES   PAGE

....
....
....
....

Title : ....

Author : ....

Genre : ....

Start date : ....

End date : ....

Number of pages : ....

#17

BOOK FORMAT

◯ Physical book

◯ E-book

◯ Audio-book

MY REVIEW

....

....

....

....

....

....

....

....

....

....

....

....

....

....

....

TYPE OF BOOK

◯ fiction

◯ Non-fiction

WHY I READ IT

....

....

WHO WILL I RECOMMEND IT TO

....

....

RATING

☆ ☆ ☆ ☆ ☆

FAVORITE QUOTES   PAGE

....

....

....

....

Title : ....

Author : ....

Genre : ....

Start date : ....

End date : ....

Number of pages : ....

BOOK FORMAT

◯ Physical book

◯ E-book

◯ Audio-book

MY REVIEW

....

....

....

....

....

....

....

....

....

....

....

....

....

....

TYPE OF BOOK

◯ fiction

◯ Non-fiction

WHY I READ IT

....

....

WHO WILL I RECOMMEND IT TO

....

....

RATING

☆ ☆ ☆ ☆ ☆

FAVORITE QUOTES   PAGE

....

....

....

....

Title : ....

Author : ....

Genre : ....

Start date : ....

End date : ....

Number of pages : ....

#19

BOOK FORMAT

◯ Physical book

◯ E-book

◯ Audio-book

MY REVIEW

....

....

....

....

....

....

....

....

....

....

....

....

....

....

TYPE OF BOOK

◯ fiction

◯ Non-fiction

WHY I READ IT

....

....

WHO WILL I RECOMMEND IT TO

....

....

RATING

☆ ☆ ☆ ☆

FAVORITE QUOTES   PAGE

....

....

....

....

Title : ....

Author : ....

Genre : ....

Start date : ....

End date : ....

Number of pages : ....

#20

BOOK FORMAT

◯ Physical book

◯ E-book

◯ Audio-book

MY REVIEW

....

....

....

....

....

....

....

....

....

....

....

....

....

TYPE OF BOOK

◯ fiction

◯ Non-fiction

WHY I READ IT

....

....

WHO WILL I RECOMMEND IT TO

....

....

RATING

☆☆☆☆☆

FAVORITE QUOTES   PAGE

....

....

....

....

Title : ....

Author : ....

Genre : ....

Start date : ....

End date : ....

Number of pages : ....

#21

BOOK FORMAT

○ Physical book

○ E-book

○ Audio-book

MY REVIEW

....

....

....

....

....

....

....

....

....

....

....

....

....

....

TYPE OF BOOK

○ fiction

○ Non-fiction

WHY I READ IT

....

....

WHO WILL I RECOMMEND IT TO

....

....

RATING

☆ ☆ ☆ ☆ ☆

FAVORITE QUOTES   PAGE

....

....

....

....

Title : ....

Author : ....

Genre : ....

Start date : ....

End date : ....

Number of pages : ....

#22

BOOK FORMAT

◯ Physical book

◯ E-book

◯ Audio-book

MY REVIEW

....

....

....

....

....

....

....

....

....

....

....

....

....

....

TYPE OF BOOK

◯ fiction

◯ Non-fiction

WHY I READ IT

....

....

WHO WILL I RECOMMEND IT TO

....

....

RATING

☆ ☆ ☆ ☆ ☆

FAVORITE QUOTES   PAGE

....

....

....

....

Title : ....

Author : ....

Genre : ....

Start date : ....

End date : ....

Number of pages : ....

#23

BOOK FORMAT

◯ Physical book

◯ E-book

◯ Audio-book

MY REVIEW

....

....

....

....

....

....

....

....

....

....

....

....

....

....

TYPE OF BOOK

◯ fiction

◯ Non-fiction

WHY I READ IT

....

....

WHO WILL I RECOMMEND IT TO

....

....

RATING

☆ ☆ ☆ ☆ ☆

FAVORITE QUOTES   PAGE :

....

....

....

....

Title : ....

Author : ....

Genre : ....

Start date : ....

End date : ....

Number of pages : ....

#24

BOOK FORMAT

◯ Physical book

◯ E-book

◯ Audio-book

MY REVIEW

....

....

....

....

....

....

....

....

....

....

....

....

....

....

TYPE OF BOOK

◯ fiction

◯ Non-fiction

WHY I READ IT

....

....

WHO WILL I RECOMMEND IT TO

....

....

RATING

☆ ☆ ☆ ☆ ☆

FAVORITE QUOTES   PAGE

....

....

....

....

Title : ....

Author : ....

Genre : ....

Start date : ....

End date : ....

Number of pages : ....

BOOK FORMAT

◯ Physical book

◯ E-book

◯ Audio-book

MY REVIEW

....

....

....

....

....

....

....

....

....

....

....

....

....

TYPE OF BOOK

◯ fiction

◯ Non-fiction

WHY I READ IT

....

....

WHO WILL I RECOMMEND IT TO

....

....

RATING

☆ ☆ ☆ ☆ ☆

FAVORITE QUOTES   PAGE

....

....

....

....

Title : ....

Author : ....

Genre : ....

Start date : ....

End date : ....

Number of pages : ....

#26

BOOK FORMAT

◯ Physical book

◯ E-book

◯ Audio-book

MY REVIEW

....

....

....

....

....

....

....

....

....

....

....

....

....

TYPE OF BOOK

◯ fiction

◯ Non-fiction

WHY I READ IT

....

....

WHO WILL I RECOMMEND IT TO

....

....

RATING

☆ ☆ ☆ ☆ ☆

FAVORITE QUOTES	PAGE #
....	....
....	....
....	....
....	....

Title : ....

Author : ....

Genre : ....

Start date : ....

End date : ....

Number of pages : ....

#27

BOOK FORMAT

◯ Physical book

◯ E-book

◯ Audio-book

TYPE OF BOOK

◯ fiction

◯ Non-fiction

WHY I READ IT

....

....

WHO WILL I RECOMMEND IT TO

....

....

RATING

☆ ☆ ☆ ☆ ☆

MY REVIEW

....

....

....

....

....

....

....

....

....

....

....

....

....

....

FAVORITE QUOTES   PAGE

....

....

....

....

Title : ....

Author : ....

Genre : ....

Start date : ....

End date : ....

Number of pages : ....

#28

BOOK FORMAT
( ) Physical book
( ) E-book
( ) Audio-book

MY REVIEW

....

....

....

....

....

....

....

....

....

....

....

....

....

TYPE OF BOOK
( ) fiction
( ) Non-fiction

WHY I READ IT
....
....

WHO WILL I RECOMMEND IT TO
....
....

RATING
☆ ☆ ☆ ☆ ☆

FAVORITE QUOTES   PAGE

....

....

....

....

Title :

Author :

Genre :

Start date :

End date :

Number of pages :

#29

BOOK FORMAT

◯ Physical book

◯ E-book

◯ Audio-book

MY REVIEW

TYPE OF BOOK

◯ fiction

◯ Non-fiction

WHY I READ IT

WHO WILL I
RECOMMEND IT TO

RATING

☆ ☆ ☆ ☆ ☆

FAVORITE QUOTES   PAGE

Title : ....

Author : ....

Genre : ....

Start date : ....

End date : ....

Number of pages : ....

#30

BOOK FORMAT

◯ Physical book

◯ E-book

◯ Audio-book

MY REVIEW

....

....

....

....

....

....

....

....

....

....

....

....

....

....

TYPE OF BOOK

◯ fiction

◯ Non-fiction

WHY I READ IT

....

....

WHO WILL I RECOMMEND IT TO

....

....

RATING

☆☆☆☆☆

FAVORITE QUOTES   PAGE

....

....

....

....

Title : ....

Author : ....

Genre : ....

Start date : ....

End date : ....

Number of pages : ....

#31

BOOK FORMAT

◯ Physical book

◯ E-book

◯ Audio-book

MY REVIEW

....

....

....

....

....

....

....

....

....

....

....

....

....

....

TYPE OF BOOK

◯ fiction

◯ Non-fiction

WHY I READ IT

....

....

WHO WILL I RECOMMEND IT TO

....

....

RATING

☆ ☆ ☆ ☆

FAVORITE QUOTES   PAGE :

....

....

....

....

Title : ....

Author : ....

Genre : ....

Start date : ....

End date : ....

Number of pages : ....

#32

BOOK FORMAT

◯ Physical book

◯ E-book

◯ Audio-book

MY REVIEW

....

....

....

....

....

....

....

....

....

....

....

....

....

....

TYPE OF BOOK

◯ fiction

◯ Non-fiction

WHY I READ IT

....

....

WHO WILL I RECOMMEND IT TO

....

....

RATING

☆ ☆ ☆ ☆ ☆

FAVORITE QUOTES   PAGE

....

....

....

....

Title : ....

#33

Author : ....

Genre : ....

BOOK FORMAT

Start date : ....

○ Physical book

End date : ....

○ E-book

Number of pages : ....

○ Audio-book

TYPE OF BOOK

....

○ fiction

....

○ Non-fiction

....

....

WHY I READ IT

....

....

....

....

....

....

WHO WILL I RECOMMEND IT TO

....

....

....

....

....

....

RATING

....

☆☆☆☆☆

....

FAVORITE QUOTES

PAGE :

....

....

....

....

Title : ....

Author : ....

Genre : ....

Start date : ....

End date : ....

Number of pages : ....

#34

BOOK FORMAT
- ◯ Physical book
- ◯ E-book
- ◯ Audio-book

MY REVIEW

....

....

....

....

....

....

....

....

....

....

....

....

....

....

....

TYPE OF BOOK
- ◯ fiction
- ◯ Non-fiction

WHY I READ IT
....
....

WHO WILL I RECOMMEND IT TO
....
....

RATING
☆ ☆ ☆ ☆ ☆

FAVORITE QUOTES   PAGE

....

....

....

....

Title : ....

Author : ....

Genre : ....

Start date : ....

End date : ....

Number of pages : ....

#35

BOOK FORMAT

◯ Physical book

◯ E-book

◯ Audio-book

TYPE OF BOOK

◯ fiction

◯ Non-fiction

MY REVIEW

....

....

....

....

....

....

....

....

....

....

....

....

....

....

WHY I READ IT

....

....

WHO WILL I RECOMMEND IT TO

....

....

RATING

☆ ☆ ☆ ☆ ☆

FAVORITE QUOTES   PAGE

....

....

....

....

Title : ....

#36

Author : ....

Genre : ....

BOOK FORMAT

Start date : ....

◯ Physical book

End date : ....

◯ E-book

Number of pages : ....

◯ Audio-book

MY REVIEW

....

TYPE OF BOOK

....

◯ fiction

....

◯ Non-fiction

....

....

....

WHY I READ IT

....

....

....

....

....

WHO WILL I RECOMMEND IT TO

....

....

....

....

....

RATING

....

☆ ☆ ☆ ☆ ☆

FAVORITE QUOTES

PAGE #

....

....

....

....

Title : ....

Author : ....

Genre : ....

Start date : ....

End date : ....

Number of pages : ....

#37

BOOK FORMAT

◯ Physical book

◯ E-book

◯ Audio-book

MY REVIEW

....

....

....

....

....

....

....

....

....

....

....

....

....

....

....

TYPE OF BOOK

◯ fiction

◯ Non-fiction

WHY I READ IT

....

....

WHO WILL I RECOMMEND IT TO

....

....

RATING

☆ ☆ ☆ ☆ ☆

FAVORITE QUOTES   PAGE

....

....

....

....

Title : ....

Author : ....

Genre : ....

Start date : ....

End date : ....

Number of pages : ....

#38

BOOK FORMAT

◯ Physical book

◯ E-book

◯ Audio-book

TYPE OF BOOK

◯ fiction

◯ Non-fiction

WHY I READ IT

....

....

WHO WILL I RECOMMEND IT TO

....

....

RATING

☆☆☆☆☆

MY REVIEW

....

....

....

....

....

....

....

....

....

....

....

....

....

....

....

FAVORITE QUOTES	PAGE #
....	....
....	....
....	....
....	....

Title : ....

Author : ....

Genre : ....

Start date : ....

End date : ....

Number of pages : ....

#39

BOOK FORMAT

◯ Physical book

◯ E-book

◯ Audio-book

MY REVIEW

....

....

....

....

....

....

....

....

....

....

....

....

....

TYPE OF BOOK

◯ fiction

◯ Non-fiction

WHY I READ IT

....

....

WHO WILL I RECOMMEND IT TO

....

....

RATING

☆ ☆ ☆ ☆ ☆

FAVORITE QUOTES   PAGE

....

....

....

....

Title : ....

Author : ....

Genre : ....

Start date : ....

End date : ....

Number of pages : ....

#40

BOOK FORMAT

◯ Physical book

◯ E-book

◯ Audio-book

MY REVIEW

....

....

....

....

....

....

....

....

....

....

....

....

....

....

....

TYPE OF BOOK

◯ fiction

◯ Non-fiction

WHY I READ IT

....

....

WHO WILL I RECOMMEND IT TO

....

....

RATING

☆ ☆ ☆ ☆ ☆

FAVORITE QUOTES   PAGE

....

....

....

....

Title : ....

Author : ....

Genre : ....

Start date : ....

End date : ....

Number of pages : ....

#41

BOOK FORMAT

◯ Physical book

◯ E-book

◯ Audio-book

MY REVIEW

....

....

....

....

....

....

....

....

....

....

....

....

....

....

TYPE OF BOOK

◯ fiction

◯ Non-fiction

WHY I READ IT

....

....

WHO WILL I RECOMMEND IT TO

....

....

RATING

☆ ☆ ☆ ☆ ☆

FAVORITE QUOTES

PAGE :

....

....

....

....

Title : ....

Author : ....

Genre : ....

Start date : ....

End date : ....

Number of pages : ....

#42

BOOK FORMAT

◯ Physical book

◯ E-book

◯ Audio-book

MY REVIEW

....

....

....

....

....

....

....

....

....

....

....

....

....

....

TYPE OF BOOK

◯ fiction

◯ Non-fiction

WHY I READ IT

....

....

WHO WILL I RECOMMEND IT TO

....

....

RATING

☆ ☆ ☆ ☆ ☆

FAVORITE QUOTES   PAGE

....

....

....

....

Title : ....

Author : ....

Genre : ....

Start date : ....

End date : ....

Number of pages : ....

BOOK FORMAT

◯ Physical book

◯ E-book

◯ Audio-book

MY REVIEW

....

....

....

....

....

....

....

....

....

....

....

....

....

....

....

TYPE OF BOOK

◯ fiction

◯ Non-fiction

WHY I READ IT

....

....

WHO WILL I RECOMMEND IT TO

....

....

RATING

☆ ☆ ☆ ☆ ☆

FAVORITE QUOTES   PAGE

....

....

....

....

Title : ....

Author : ....

Genre : ....

Start date : ....

End date : ....

Number of pages : ....

#44

BOOK FORMAT

◯ Physical book

◯ E-book

◯ Audio-book

MY REVIEW

....

....

....

....

....

....

....

....

....

....

....

....

....

....

TYPE OF BOOK

◯ fiction

◯ Non-fiction

WHY I READ IT

....

....

WHO WILL I RECOMMEND IT TO

....

....

RATING

☆ ☆ ☆ ☆ ☆

FAVORITE QUOTES   PAGE

....

....

....

....

Title : ....

Author : ....

Genre : ....

Start date : ....

End date : ....

Number of pages : ....

#45

BOOK FORMAT

◯ Physical book

◯ E-book

◯ Audio-book

MY REVIEW

....

....

....

....

....

....

....

....

....

....

....

....

....

....

TYPE OF BOOK

◯ fiction

◯ Non-fiction

WHY I READ IT

....

....

WHO WILL I RECOMMEND IT TO

....

....

RATING

☆ ☆ ☆ ☆ ☆

FAVORITE QUOTES

PAGE

....

....

....

....

Title : ....

Author : ....

Genre : ....

Start date : ....

End date : ....

Number of pages : ....

BOOK FORMAT

◯ Physical book

◯ E-book

◯ Audio-book

MY REVIEW

....

....

....

....

....

....

....

....

....

....

....

....

....

....

....

TYPE OF BOOK

◯ fiction

◯ Non-fiction

WHY I READ IT

....

....

WHO WILL I RECOMMEND IT TO

....

....

RATING

☆☆☆☆☆

FAVORITE QUOTES   PAGE

....

....

....

....

Title : ....

Author : ....

Genre : ....

Start date : ....

End date : ....

Number of pages : ....

#47

BOOK FORMAT

◯ Physical book

◯ E-book

◯ Audio-book

MY REVIEW

....

....

....

....

....

....

....

....

....

....

....

....

....

....

TYPE OF BOOK

◯ fiction

◯ Non-fiction

WHY I READ IT

....

....

WHO WILL I RECOMMEND IT TO

....

....

RATING

☆ ☆ ☆ ☆ ☆

FAVORITE QUOTES   PAGE

....

....

....

....

Title : ....

Author : ....

Genre : ....

Start date : ....

End date : ....

Number of pages : ....

BOOK FORMAT

( ) Physical book

( ) E-book

( ) Audio-book

MY REVIEW

....
....
....
....
....
....
....
....
....
....
....
....
....
....

TYPE OF BOOK

( ) fiction

( ) Non-fiction

WHY I READ IT

....
....

WHO WILL I RECOMMEND IT TO

....
....

RATING

☆ ☆ ☆ ☆ ☆

FAVORITE QUOTES   PAGE

....
....
....
....

Title : ....

Author : ....

Genre : ....

Start date : ....

End date : ....

Number of pages : ....

#49

BOOK FORMAT

◯ Physical book

◯ E-book

◯ Audio-book

MY REVIEW

....
....
....
....
....
....
....
....
....
....
....
....
....
....

TYPE OF BOOK

◯ fiction

◯ Non-fiction

WHY I READ IT

....
....

WHO WILL I RECOMMEND IT TO

....
....

RATING

☆ ☆ ☆ ☆ ☆

FAVORITE QUOTES   PAGE

....

....

....

....

Title : ....

Author : ....

Genre : ....

Start date : ....

End date : ....

Number of pages : ....

#50

BOOK FORMAT

◯ Physical book

◯ E-book

◯ Audio-book

MY REVIEW

....

....

....

....

....

....

....

....

....

....

....

....

....

....

TYPE OF BOOK

◯ fiction

◯ Non-fiction

WHY I READ IT

....

....

WHO WILL I RECOMMEND IT TO

....

....

RATING

☆ ☆ ☆ ☆ ☆

FAVORITE QUOTES   PAGE

....

....

....

....

Title : ....

Author : ....

Genre : ....

Start date : ....

End date : ....

Number of pages : ....

#51

BOOK FORMAT

◯ Physical book

◯ E-book

◯ Audio-book

TYPE OF BOOK

◯ fiction

◯ Non-fiction

MY REVIEW

....

....

....

....

....

....

....

....

....

....

....

....

....

....

....

WHY I READ IT

....

....

WHO WILL I RECOMMEND IT TO

....

....

RATING

☆ ☆ ☆ ☆ ☆

FAVORITE QUOTES	PAGE
....	....
....	....
....	....
....	....

Title : ....

Author : ....

Genre : ....

Start date : ....

End date : ....

Number of pages : ....

#52

BOOK FORMAT

◯ Physical book

◯ E-book

◯ Audio-book

MY REVIEW

....

....

....

....

....

....

....

....

....

....

....

....

....

....

TYPE OF BOOK

◯ fiction

◯ Non-fiction

WHY I READ IT

....

....

WHO WILL I RECOMMEND IT TO

....

....

RATING

☆ ☆ ☆ ☆ ☆

FAVORITE QUOTES

PAGE #

....

....

....

....

Title : ....

Author : ....

Genre : ....

Start date : ....

End date : ....

Number of pages : ....

#53

BOOK FORMAT

◯ Physical book

◯ E-book

◯ Audio-book

MY REVIEW

....

....

....

....

....

....

....

....

....

....

....

....

....

TYPE OF BOOK

◯ fiction

◯ Non-fiction

WHY I READ IT

....

....

WHO WILL I RECOMMEND IT T

....

....

RATING

☆ ☆ ☆ ☆ ☆

FAVORITE QUOTES   PAGE

....

....

....

....

Title : ....

Author : ....

Genre : ....

Start date : ....

End date : ....

Number of pages : ....

#54

BOOK FORMAT

◯ Physical book

◯ E-book

◯ Audio-book

MY REVIEW

....

....

....

....

....

....

....

....

....

....

....

....

....

....

TYPE OF BOOK

◯ fiction

◯ Non-fiction

WHY I READ IT

....

....

WHO WILL I RECOMMEND IT TO

....

....

RATING

☆ ☆ ☆ ☆ ☆

FAVORITE QUOTES   PAGE

....

....

....

....

Title : ....

Author : ....

Genre : ....

Start date : ....

End date : ....

Number of pages : ....

#55

BOOK FORMAT

◯ Physical book

◯ E-book

◯ Audio-book

MY REVIEW

....

....

....

....

....

....

....

....

....

....

....

....

....

....

TYPE OF BOOK

◯ fiction

◯ Non-fiction

WHY I READ IT

....

....

WHO WILL I RECOMMEND IT T-

....

....

RATING

☆ ☆ ☆ ☆ ☆

FAVORITE QUOTES   PAGE

....

....

....

....

Title : ....

Author : ....

Genre : ....

Start date : ....

End date : ....

Number of pages : ....

#56

BOOK FORMAT

◯ Physical book

◯ E-book

◯ Audio-book

MY REVIEW

....

....

....

....

....

....

....

....

....

....

....

....

....

TYPE OF BOOK

◯ fiction

◯ Non-fiction

WHY I READ IT

....

....

WHO WILL I RECOMMEND IT TO

....

....

RATING

☆☆☆☆☆

FAVORITE QUOTES   PAGE

....

....

....

....

Title : ....

Author : ....

Genre : ....

Start date : ....

End date : ....

Number of pages : ....

#57

BOOK FORMAT

◯ Physical book

◯ E-book

◯ Audio-book

MY REVIEW

....

....

....

....

....

....

....

....

....

....

....

....

....

....

TYPE OF BOOK

◯ fiction

◯ Non-fiction

WHY I READ IT

....

....

WHO WILL I RECOMMEND IT T

....

....

RATING

☆☆☆☆☆

FAVORITE QUOTES   PAGE

....

....

....

....

Title : ....

Author : ....

Genre : ....

Start date : ....

End date : ....

Number of pages : ....

#58

BOOK FORMAT

◯ Physical book

◯ E-book

◯ Audio-book

MY REVIEW

....

....

....

....

....

....

....

....

....

....

....

....

....

....

TYPE OF BOOK

◯ fiction

◯ Non-fiction

WHY I READ IT

....

....

WHO WILL I RECOMMEND IT TO

....

....

RATING

☆☆☆☆☆

FAVORITE QUOTES

PAGE #

....

....

....

....

Title : ....

Author : ....

Genre : ....

Start date : ....

End date : ....

Number of pages : ....

#59

BOOK FORMAT

◯ Physical book

◯ E-book

◯ Audio-book

MY REVIEW

....
....
....
....
....
....
....
....
....
....
....
....
....
....

TYPE OF BOOK

◯ fiction

◯ Non-fiction

WHY I READ IT

....
....

WHO WILL I RECOMMEND IT T

....
....

RATING

☆ ☆ ☆ ☆ ☆

FAVORITE QUOTES   PAGE

....
....
....
....

Title : ....

Author : ....

Genre : ....

Start date : ....

End date : ....

Number of pages : ....

#60

BOOK FORMAT

◯ Physical book

◯ E-book

◯ Audio-book

MY REVIEW

....

....

....

....

....

....

....

....

....

....

....

....

....

TYPE OF BOOK

◯ fiction

◯ Non-fiction

WHY I READ IT

....

....

WHO WILL I RECOMMEND IT TO

....

....

RATING

☆ ☆ ☆ ☆ ☆

FAVORITE QUOTES   PAGE

....

....

....

....

Title : ....

Author : ....

Genre : ....

Start date : ....

End date : ....

Number of pages : ....

#61

BOOK FORMAT

◯ Physical book

◯ E-book

◯ Audio-book

MY REVIEW

....

....

....

....

....

....

....

....

....

....

....

....

....

....

TYPE OF BOOK

◯ fiction

◯ Non-fiction

WHY I READ IT

....

....

WHO WILL I RECOMMEND IT T

....

....

RATING

☆ ☆ ☆ ☆ ☆

FAVORITE QUOTES   PAGE

....

....

....

....

Title : ....

Author : ....

Genre : ....

Start date : ....

End date : ....

Number of pages : ....

#62

BOOK FORMAT

◯ Physical book

◯ E-book

◯ Audio-book

MY REVIEW

....

....

....

....

....

....

....

....

....

....

....

....

....

....

....

TYPE OF BOOK

◯ fiction

◯ Non-fiction

WHY I READ IT

....

....

WHO WILL I RECOMMEND IT TO

....

....

RATING

☆☆☆☆☆

FAVORITE QUOTES   PAGE

....

....

....

....

Title : ....

Author : ....

Genre : ....

Start date : ....

End date : ....

Number of pages : ....

#63

BOOK FORMAT

◯ Physical book

◯ E-book

◯ Audio-book

MY REVIEW

....
....
....
....
....
....
....
....
....
....
....
....
....
....

TYPE OF BOOK

◯ fiction

◯ Non-fiction

WHY I READ IT

....
....

WHO WILL I RECOMMEND IT T

....
....

RATING

☆☆☆☆☆

FAVORITE QUOTES   PAGE

....
....
....
....

Title : ....

Author : ....

Genre : ....

Start date : ....

End date : ....

Number of pages : ....

#64

BOOK FORMAT

◯ Physical book

◯ E-book

◯ Audio-book

MY REVIEW

....

....

....

....

....

....

....

....

....

....

....

....

....

....

....

TYPE OF BOOK

◯ fiction

◯ Non-fiction

WHY I READ IT

....

....

WHO WILL I RECOMMEND IT TO

....

....

RATING

☆ ☆ ☆ ☆ ☆

FAVORITE QUOTES   PAGE

....

....

....

....

Title : ....

Author : ....

Genre : ....

Start date : ....

End date : ....

Number of pages : ....

#65

BOOK FORMAT

◯ Physical book

◯ E-book

◯ Audio-book

MY REVIEW

....

....

....

....

....

....

....

....

....

....

....

....

....

....

TYPE OF BOOK

◯ fiction

◯ Non-fiction

WHY I READ IT

....

....

WHO WILL I RECOMMEND IT T

....

....

RATING

☆☆☆☆☆

FAVORITE QUOTES   PAGE

....

....

....

....

Title : ....

Author : ....

Genre : ....

Start date : ....

End date : ....

Number of pages : ....

#66

BOOK FORMAT

◯ Physical book

◯ E-book

◯ Audio-book

MY REVIEW

....
....
....
....
....
....
....
....
....
....
....
....
....

TYPE OF BOOK

◯ fiction

◯ Non-fiction

WHY I READ IT

....
....

WHO WILL I RECOMMEND IT TO

....
....

RATING

☆ ☆ ☆ ☆ ☆

FAVORITE QUOTES   PAGE

....

....

....

....

Title : ....

Author : ....

Genre : ....

Start date : ....

End date : ....

Number of pages : ....

#67

BOOK FORMAT

◯ Physical book

◯ E-book

◯ Audio-book

MY REVIEW

....

....

....

....

....

....

....

....

....

....

....

....

....

....

....

TYPE OF BOOK

◯ fiction

◯ Non-fiction

WHY I READ IT

....

....

WHO WILL I RECOMMEND IT T

....

....

RATING

☆☆☆☆☆

FAVORITE QUOTES   PAGE

....

....

....

....

Title : ....

Author : ....

Genre : ....

Start date : ....

End date : ....

Number of pages : ....

#68

BOOK FORMAT

◯ Physical book

◯ E-book

◯ Audio-book

MY REVIEW

....

....

....

....

....

....

....

....

....

....

....

....

....

....

TYPE OF BOOK

◯ fiction

◯ Non-fiction

WHY I READ IT

....

....

WHO WILL I RECOMMEND IT TO

....

....

RATING

☆☆☆☆☆

FAVORITE QUOTES

PAGE #

....

....

....

....

Title : ....

Author : ....

Genre : ....

Start date : ....

End date : ....

Number of pages : ....

#69

BOOK FORMAT

◯ Physical book

◯ E-book

◯ Audio-book

MY REVIEW

....

....

....

....

....

....

....

....

....

....

....

....

....

....

TYPE OF BOOK

◯ fiction

◯ Non-fiction

WHY I READ IT

....

....

WHO WILL I RECOMMEND IT T

....

....

RATING

☆☆☆☆☆

FAVORITE QUOTES	PAGE
....	....
....	....
....	....
....	....

Title : ....

Author : ....

Genre : ....

Start date : ....

End date : ....

Number of pages : ....

#70

BOOK FORMAT

- ◯ Physical book
- ◯ E-book
- ◯ Audio-book

MY REVIEW

....

....

....

....

....

....

....

....

....

....

....

....

....

....

TYPE OF BOOK

- ◯ fiction
- ◯ Non-fiction

WHY I READ IT

....

....

WHO WILL I RECOMMEND IT TO

....

....

RATING

☆ ☆ ☆ ☆ ☆

FAVORITE QUOTES   PAGE

....

....

....

....

Title : ....

Author : ....

Genre : ....

Start date : ....

End date : ....

Number of pages : ....

#71

BOOK FORMAT

○ Physical book

○ E-book

○ Audio-book

MY REVIEW

....

....

....

....

....

....

....

....

....

....

....

....

....

....

TYPE OF BOOK

○ fiction

○ Non-fiction

WHY I READ IT

....

....

WHO WILL I RECOMMEND IT T

....

....

RATING

☆☆☆☆☆

FAVORITE QUOTES   PAGE

....

....

....

....

Title : ....

Author : ....

Genre : ....

Start date : ....

End date : ....

Number of pages : ....

#72

BOOK FORMAT

◯ Physical book

◯ E-book

◯ Audio-book

MY REVIEW

....

....

....

....

....

....

....

....

....

....

....

....

....

....

TYPE OF BOOK

◯ fiction

◯ Non-fiction

WHY I READ IT

....

....

WHO WILL I RECOMMEND IT TO

....

....

RATING

☆☆☆☆☆

FAVORITE QUOTES   PAGE

....

....

....

....

Title : ....

Author : ....

Genre : ....

Start date : ....

End date : ....

Number of pages : ....

#73

BOOK FORMAT

◯ Physical book

◯ E-book

◯ Audio-book

MY REVIEW

....

....

....

....

....

....

....

....

....

....

....

....

....

....

TYPE OF BOOK

◯ fiction

◯ Non-fiction

WHY I READ IT

....

....

WHO WILL I RECOMMEND IT T

....

....

RATING

☆☆☆☆☆

FAVORITE QUOTES   PAGE

....

....

....

....

Title : ....

Author : ....

Genre : ....

Start date : ....

End date : ....

Number of pages : ....

#74

BOOK FORMAT

◯ Physical book

◯ E-book

◯ Audio-book

MY REVIEW

....

....

....

....

....

....

....

....

....

....

....

....

....

TYPE OF BOOK

◯ fiction

◯ Non-fiction

WHY I READ IT

....

....

WHO WILL I RECOMMEND IT TO

....

....

RATING

☆ ☆ ☆ ☆ ☆

FAVORITE QUOTES   PAGE

....

....

....

....

Title : ....

Author : ....

Genre : ....

Start date : ....

End date : ....

Number of pages : ....

#75

BOOK FORMAT

◯ Physical book

◯ E-book

◯ Audio-book

MY REVIEW

....

....

....

....

....

....

....

....

....

....

....

....

....

....

TYPE OF BOOK

◯ fiction

◯ Non-fiction

WHY I READ IT

....

....

WHO WILL I RECOMMEND IT T

....

....

RATING

☆☆☆☆☆

FAVORITE QUOTES   PAGE

....

....

....

....

Title : ....

Author : ....

Genre : ....

Start date : ....

End date : ....

Number of pages : ....

#76

BOOK FORMAT

◯ Physical book

◯ E-book

◯ Audio-book

MY REVIEW

....

....

....

....

....

....

....

....

....

....

....

....

....

TYPE OF BOOK

◯ fiction

◯ Non-fiction

WHY I READ IT

....

....

WHO WILL I RECOMMEND IT TO

....

....

RATING

☆☆☆☆☆

FAVORITE QUOTES   PAGE

....

....

....

....

Title : ....

Author : ....

Genre : ....

Start date : ....

End date : ....

Number of pages : ....

#77

BOOK FORMAT

◯ Physical book

◯ E-book

◯ Audio-book

MY REVIEW

....

....

....

....

....

....

....

....

....

....

....

....

....

TYPE OF BOOK

◯ fiction

◯ Non-fiction

WHY I READ IT

....

....

WHO WILL I RECOMMEND IT T

....

....

RATING

☆ ☆ ☆ ☆ ☆

FAVORITE QUOTES   PAGE

....

....

....

....

Title : ....

Author : ....

Genre : ....

Start date : ....

End date : ....

Number of pages : ....

#78

BOOK FORMAT

( ) Physical book

( ) E-book

( ) Audio-book

MY REVIEW

....

....

....

....

....

....

....

....

....

....

....

....

....

....

TYPE OF BOOK

( ) fiction

( ) Non-fiction

WHY I READ IT

....

....

WHO WILL I RECOMMEND IT TO

....

....

RATING

☆☆☆☆☆

FAVORITE QUOTES

PAGE #

....

....

....

....

Title : ....

Author : ....

Genre : ....

Start date : ....

End date : ....

Number of pages : ....

#79

BOOK FORMAT

○ Physical book

○ E-book

○ Audio-book

MY REVIEW

....

....

....

....

....

....

....

....

....

....

....

....

....

....

....

TYPE OF BOOK

○ fiction

○ Non-fiction

WHY I READ IT

....

....

WHO WILL I RECOMMEND IT T

....

....

RATING

☆ ☆ ☆ ☆ ☆

FAVORITE QUOTES   PAGE

....

....

....

....

Title : ....

Author : ....

Genre : ....

Start date : ....

End date : ....

Number of pages : ....

#80

BOOK FORMAT

◯ Physical book

◯ E-book

◯ Audio-book

MY REVIEW

....

....

....

....

....

....

....

....

....

....

....

....

....

....

TYPE OF BOOK

◯ fiction

◯ Non-fiction

WHY I READ IT

....

....

WHO WILL I RECOMMEND IT TO

....

....

RATING

☆ ☆ ☆ ☆ ☆

FAVORITE QUOTES   PAGE

....

....

....

....

Title : ....

Author : ....

Genre : ....

Start date : ....

End date : ....

Number of pages : ....

#81

BOOK FORMAT

- ◯ Physical book
- ◯ E-book
- ◯ Audio-book

MY REVIEW

....

....

....

....

....

....

....

....

....

....

....

....

....

....

TYPE OF BOOK

- ◯ fiction
- ◯ Non-fiction

WHY I READ IT

....

....

WHO WILL I RECOMMEND IT T

....

....

RATING

☆☆☆☆☆

FAVORITE QUOTES	PAGE
....	....
....	....
....	....
....	....

Title : ....

Author : ....

Genre : ....

Start date : ....

End date : ....

Number of pages : ....

#82

BOOK FORMAT

○ Physical book

○ E-book

○ Audio-book

MY REVIEW

....

....

....

....

....

....

....

....

....

....

....

....

....

....

....

TYPE OF BOOK

○ fiction

○ Non-fiction

WHY I READ IT

....

....

WHO WILL I RECOMMEND IT TO

....

....

RATING

☆ ☆ ☆ ☆ ☆

FAVORITE QUOTES

....

....

....

....

PAGE

Title : ....

#83

Author : ....

Genre : ....

Start date : ....

End date : ....

Number of pages : ....

MY REVIEW

....
....
....
....
....
....
....
....
....
....
....
....
....
....

TYPE OF BOOK

◯ fiction
◯ Non-fiction

WHY I READ IT

....
....

WHO WILL I
RECOMMEND IT T

....
....

RATING

☆☆☆☆☆

FAVORITE QUOTES   PAGE

....
....
....
....

Title : ....

Author : ....

Genre : ....

Start date : ....

End date : ....

Number of pages : ....

#84

BOOK FORMAT

◯ Physical book

◯ E-book

◯ Audio-book

MY REVIEW

....
....
....
....
....
....
....
....
....
....
....
....
....
....
....
....

TYPE OF BOOK

◯ fiction

◯ Non-fiction

WHY I READ IT

....
....

WHO WILL I RECOMMEND IT TO

....
....

RATING

☆☆☆☆☆

FAVORITE QUOTES

	PAGE #
....	....
....	....
....	....
....	....

Title : ....

Author : ....

Genre : ....

Start date : ....

End date : ....

Number of pages : ....

#85

BOOK FORMAT

○ Physical book

○ E-book

○ Audio-book

MY REVIEW

....

....

....

....

....

....

....

....

....

....

....

....

....

....

....

TYPE OF BOOK

○ fiction

○ Non-fiction

WHY I READ IT

....

....

WHO WILL I RECOMMEND IT T

....

....

RATING

☆☆☆☆☆

FAVORITE QUOTES   PAGE

....

....

....

....

Title : ....

Author : ....

Genre : ....

Start date : ....

End date : ....

Number of pages : ....

#86

BOOK FORMAT

◯ Physical book

◯ E-book

◯ Audio-book

MY REVIEW

....

....

....

....

....

....

....

....

....

....

....

....

TYPE OF BOOK

◯ fiction

◯ Non-fiction

WHY I READ IT

....

....

WHO WILL I RECOMMEND IT TO

....

....

RATING

☆ ☆ ☆ ☆ ☆

FAVORITE QUOTES

PAGE

....

....

....

....

Title : ....

Author : ....

Genre : ....

Start date : ....

End date : ....

Number of pages : ....

#87

BOOK FORMAT

◯ Physical book

◯ E-book

◯ Audio-book

MY REVIEW

....

....

....

....

....

....

....

....

....

....

....

....

....

....

TYPE OF BOOK

◯ fiction

◯ Non-fiction

WHY I READ IT

....

....

WHO WILL I RECOMMEND IT T

....

....

RATING

☆ ☆ ☆ ☆ ☆

FAVORITE QUOTES   PAGE

....

....

....

....

Title : ....

Author : ....

Genre : ....

Start date : ....

End date : ....

Number of pages : ....

#88

BOOK FORMAT

◯ Physical book

◯ E-book

◯ Audio-book

MY REVIEW

....

....

....

....

....

....

....

....

....

....

....

....

....

....

TYPE OF BOOK

◯ fiction

◯ Non-fiction

WHY I READ IT

....

....

WHO WILL I RECOMMEND IT TO

....

....

RATING

☆☆☆☆☆

FAVORITE QUOTES   PAGE

....

....

....

....

Title : ....

Author : ....

Genre : ....

Start date : ....

End date : ....

Number of pages : ....

MY REVIEW

....

....

....

....

....

....

....

....

....

....

....

....

....

BOOK FORMAT

◯ Physical book

◯ E-book

◯ Audio-book

TYPE OF BOOK

◯ fiction

◯ Non-fiction

WHY I READ IT

....

....

WHO WILL I RECOMMEND IT T

....

....

RATING

☆☆☆☆☆

FAVORITE QUOTES   PAGE

....

....

....

....

Title : .... **#90**

Author : ....

Genre : ....

Start date : ....

End date : ....

Number of pages : ....

BOOK FORMAT

( ) Physical book

( ) E-book

( ) Audio-book

MY REVIEW

....

....

....

....

....

....

....

....

....

....

....

....

....

....

TYPE OF BOOK

( ) fiction

( ) Non-fiction

WHY I READ IT

....

....

WHO WILL I RECOMMEND IT TO

....

....

RATING

☆ ☆ ☆ ☆ ☆

FAVORITE QUOTES

PAGE #

....

....

....

....

Title : ....

Author : ....

Genre : ....

Start date : ....

End date : ....

Number of pages : ....

#91

BOOK FORMAT

◯ Physical book

◯ E-book

◯ Audio-book

MY REVIEW

....

....

....

....

....

....

....

....

....

....

....

....

....

....

TYPE OF BOOK

◯ fiction

◯ Non-fiction

WHY I READ IT

....

....

WHO WILL I RECOMMEND IT T

....

....

RATING

☆☆☆☆☆

FAVORITE QUOTES   PAGE

....

....

....

....

Title : ....

Author : ....

Genre : ....

Start date : ....

End date : ....

Number of pages : ....

#92

BOOK FORMAT

○ Physical book

○ E-book

○ Audio-book

MY REVIEW

....

....

....

....

....

....

....

....

....

....

....

....

....

....

TYPE OF BOOK

○ fiction

○ Non-fiction

WHY I READ IT

....

....

WHO WILL I RECOMMEND IT TO

....

....

RATING

☆☆☆☆☆

FAVORITE QUOTES   PAGE

....

....

....

....

Title : ....

Author : ....

Genre : ....

Start date : ....

End date : ....

Number of pages : ....

#93

BOOK FORMAT

( ) Physical book

( ) E-book

( ) Audio-book

MY REVIEW

....

....

....

....

....

....

....

....

....

....

....

....

....

TYPE OF BOOK

( ) fiction

( ) Non-fiction

WHY I READ IT

....

....

WHO WILL I RECOMMEND IT T

....

....

RATING

☆ ☆ ☆ ☆ ☆

FAVORITE QUOTES

....

....

....

....

| | PAGE |

Title : ....

Author : ....

Genre : ....

Start date : ....

End date : ....

Number of pages : ....

#94

BOOK FORMAT

◯ Physical book

◯ E-book

◯ Audio-book

MY REVIEW

....

....

....

....

....

....

....

....

....

....

....

....

....

....

....

TYPE OF BOOK

◯ fiction

◯ Non-fiction

WHY I READ IT

....

....

WHO WILL I RECOMMEND IT TO

....

....

RATING

☆☆☆☆☆

FAVORITE QUOTES

PAGE

....

....

....

....

Title : ....

Author : ....

Genre : ....

Start date : ....

End date : ....

Number of pages : ....

BOOK FORMAT

◯ Physical book

◯ E-book

◯ Audio-book

MY REVIEW

....

....

....

....

....

....

....

....

....

....

....

....

....

....

TYPE OF BOOK

◯ fiction

◯ Non-fiction

WHY I READ IT

....

....

WHO WILL I RECOMMEND IT T

....

....

RATING

☆☆☆☆☆

FAVORITE QUOTES   PAGE

....

....

....

....

Title : ....

Author : ....

Genre : ....

Start date : ....

End date : ....

Number of pages : ....

#96

BOOK FORMAT

○ Physical book

○ E-book

○ Audio-book

MY REVIEW

....

....

....

....

....

....

....

....

....

....

....

....

....

....

TYPE OF BOOK

○ fiction

○ Non-fiction

WHY I READ IT

....

....

WHO WILL I RECOMMEND IT TO

....

....

RATING

☆ ☆ ☆ ☆ ☆

FAVORITE QUOTES

PAGE #

....

....

....

....

Title : ....

Author : ....

Genre : ....

Start date : ....

End date : ....

Number of pages : ....

BOOK FORMAT

◯ Physical book

◯ E-book

◯ Audio-book

MY REVIEW

....

....

....

....

....

....

....

....

....

....

....

....

....

....

TYPE OF BOOK

◯ fiction

◯ Non-fiction

WHY I READ IT

....

....

WHO WILL I RECOMMEND IT T

....

....

RATING

☆☆☆☆☆

FAVORITE QUOTES   PAGE

....

....

....

....

Title : ....

Author : ....

Genre : ....

Start date : ....

End date : ....

Number of pages : ....

#98

BOOK FORMAT

◯ Physical book

◯ E-book

◯ Audio-book

MY REVIEW

....

....

....

....

....

....

....

....

....

....

....

....

....

....

....

TYPE OF BOOK

◯ fiction

◯ Non-fiction

WHY I READ IT

....

....

WHO WILL I RECOMMEND IT TO

....

....

RATING

☆☆☆☆☆

FAVORITE QUOTES   PAGE

....

....

....

....

Title : ....

Author : ....

Genre : ....

Start date : ....

End date : ....

Number of pages : ....

#99

BOOK FORMAT

◯ Physical book

◯ E-book

◯ Audio-book

MY REVIEW

....

....

....

....

....

....

....

....

....

....

....

....

....

....

TYPE OF BOOK

◯ fiction

◯ Non-fiction

WHY I READ IT

....

....

WHO WILL I RECOMMEND IT T

....

....

RATING

☆☆☆☆☆

FAVORITE QUOTES   PAGE

....

....

....

....

Title : ....

Author : ....

Genre : ....

Start date : ....

End date : ....

Number of pages : ....

#100

BOOK FORMAT

◯ Physical book

◯ E-book

◯ Audio-book

MY REVIEW

....

....

....

....

....

....

....

....

....

....

....

....

....

TYPE OF BOOK

◯ fiction

◯ Non-fiction

WHY I READ IT

....

....

WHO WILL I RECOMMEND IT TO

....

....

RATING

☆☆☆☆☆

FAVORITE QUOTES

PAGE #

....

....

....

....

Made in United States
Orlando, FL
16 January 2023

28716249R00057